Using Microsoft Office 2013

With Windows 8

Kevin Wilson

Apress®

Using Microsoft Office 2013: With Windows 8

ISBN-13 (pbk): 978-1-4302-6688-4

ISBN-13 (electronic): 978-1-4302-6689-1

President and Publisher: Paul Manning

Lead Editor: Steve Anglin

Editorial Board: Steve Anglin, Mark Beckner, Ewan Buckingham, Gary Cornell, Louise Corrigan, Jonathan Gennick, Jonathan Hassell, Robert Hutchinson, Michelle Lowman, James Markham, Matthew Moodie, Jeff Olson, Jeffrey Pepper, Douglas Pundick, Ben Renow-Clarke, Dominic Shakeshaft, Gwenan Spearing, Matt Wade, Steve Weiss

Copy Editor: Vanessa Moore

Compositor: SPi Global
Indexer: SPi Global
Artist: SPi Global
Cover Designer: Anna Ishchenko

Distributed to the book trade worldwide by Springer Science+Business Media New York, 233 Spring Street, 6th Floor, New York, NY 10013. Phone 1-800-SPRINGER, fax (201) 348-4505, e-mail orders-ny@springer-sbm.com, or visit www.springeronline.com. Apress Media, LLC is a California LLC and the sole member (owner) is Springer Science + Business Media Finance Inc (SSBM Finance Inc). SSBM Finance Inc is a **Delaware** corporation.

For information on translations, please e-mail rights@apress.com, or visit www.apress.com.

Apress and friends of ED books may be purchased in bulk for academic, corporate, or promotional use. eBook versions and licenses are also available for most titles. For more information, reference our Special Bulk Sales–eBook Licensing web page at www.apress.com/bulk-sales.

Contents at a Glance

About the Author

Kevin Wilson, a practicing computer engineer and tutor, has had a passion for gadgets, cameras, computers, and technology for many years.

He graduated with masters degrees in computer science, software engineering, and multimedia systems. He has gone on to work within the computer industry, supporting and working with many different types of computer systems, as well as working within the educational system, running specialist lessons on filmmaking and visual effects for young people. He has also worked as an IT tutor, has taught in colleges in South Africa, and served as a tutor for adult education in England.

He continues to write books in the hope that his work will help people use their computers with greater understanding, productivity, and efficiency. His ultimate goal is to help students and people in countries, like South Africa, who have never used a computer before. It is his hope that they will, one day, get the same benefits from computer technology as we do.

Acknowledgments

Thanks to all the staff at Apress for their passion, dedication, and hard work in the preparation and production of this book.

To all my friends and family for their continued support and encouragement in all my writing projects.

To all my colleagues, students, and testers who took the time to test procedures and offer feedback on the book.

Finally, thanks to you, the reader, for choosing this book. I hope it helps you use your computer with greater ease.

Introduction

Using Microsoft Office 2013 introduces you to the new verson of Microsoft Office and is designed to help beginners and enthusiast users who want to get up and running quickly using their computers.

This book has been written in a step-by-step fashion, using photography and screen shots to illustrate the steps as clearly and as concisely as possible, starting with the fundamentals of what Office is. We then take a look at using the most common Office Applications, with guided tutorials on creating documents in Word with different fonts, graphics, photographs, and colors. We learn how to manipulate data in Excel to create tables, perform calculations, and create charts. We use PowerPoint to get our message across by creating multimedia presentations using graphics, photograhs, and animations. Finally we learn how to set up Outlook to check our e-mail and keep appointments and contacts.

CHAPTER 1

■ ■ ■

Microsoft Office 2013

Microsoft Office 2013 is a suite of applications that enable you to produce documents, spreadsheets, presentations and other desktop publishing.

Here is a summary of the applications available in Microsoft Office 2013:

Microsoft Office 2013 is available in three different forms which are aimed at different users.

Home & Student is aimed at ordinary home users, university and college students and contains the basic applications that most home users would use: Word, Excel, PowerPoint and OneNote.

Home & Business is more or less the same as Home & Student except it adds the Outlook e-mail application.

Office Professional is aimed at business and power users and contains all the applications you would use when working for or running a business. It includes all the applications of Home & Business but adds desktop publishing with Microsoft Publisher and a database management system for keeping records called Microsoft Access.

Product	Installs	Included Apps
Home & Student	1 PC	W X P N
Home & Business	1 PC	W X P N O
Professional	1 PC	W X P N O P A

For this guide we will be focussing on the most used office applications: Word, Excel, PowerPoint and Outlook.

Microsoft Word

Microsoft Word is a word processing program used for typing documents and desktop publishing. Users can create letters, documents, cards and more with it.

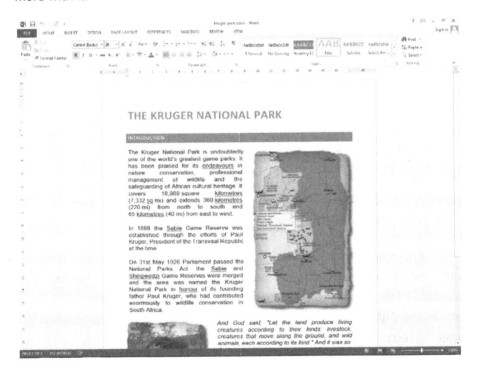

Microsoft Excel

Microsoft Excel is a spreadsheet program, used for organizing and analyzing financial data. Users can create budgets, score sheets, and various data charts with it.

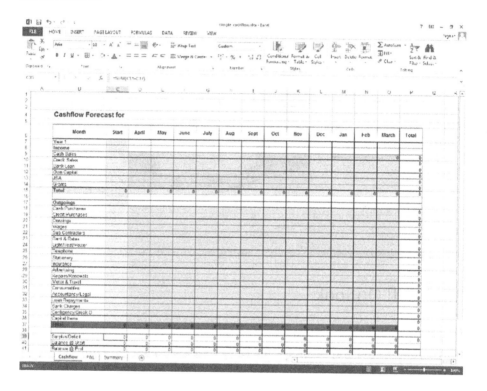

Microsoft PowerPoint

Microsoft PowerPoint is used for creating and giving presentations. It is used to create slideshows, using text and graphics, which can be displayed on-screen or shown to an audience using a projector.

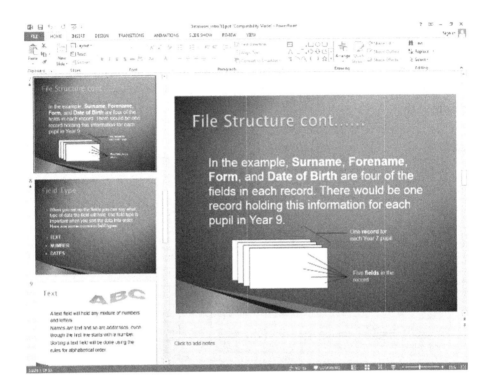

Microsoft Outlook

Microsoft Outlook is a personal information manager and e-mail system. It allows you to send and receive e-mails, as well askeep address books of contacts and record appointments on an electronic calendar.

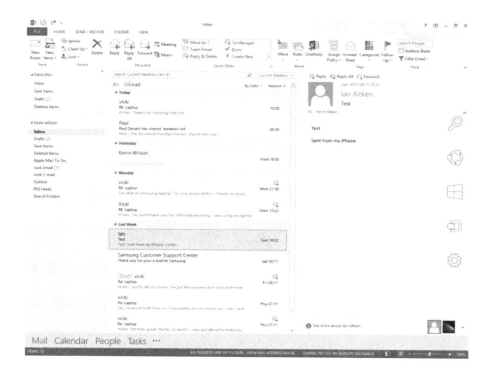

CHAPTER 2

■ ■ ■

Microsoft Word 2013

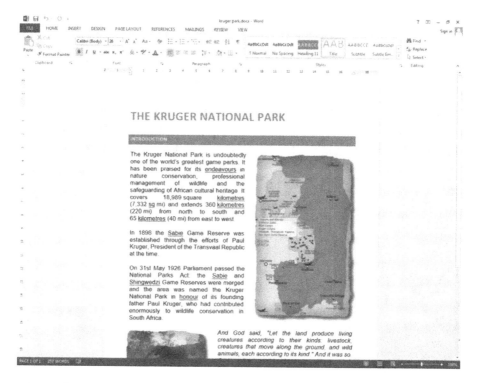

Microsoft Word allows you to create many different types of documents, from letters and resumes/CVs, to greetings cards, posters, and more.

Starting Word

To launch Word, go to the Start screen and select "Word 2013."

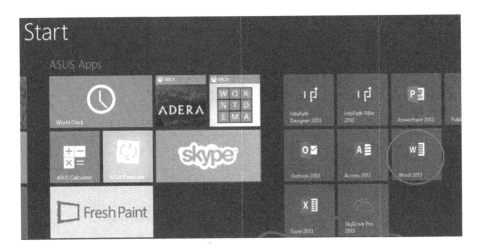

After Word has loaded, you can select a document from a wide variety of templates, such as brochures, CVs, letters, flyers, and more. If you want to create your own, just select the "Blank document." Your recently saved documents are shown in the blue pane on the left-hand side of the screen.

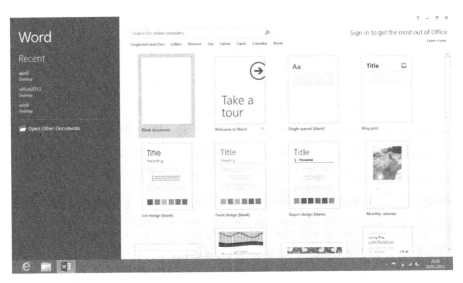

You can also search for a particular template using the search field at the top of the screen.

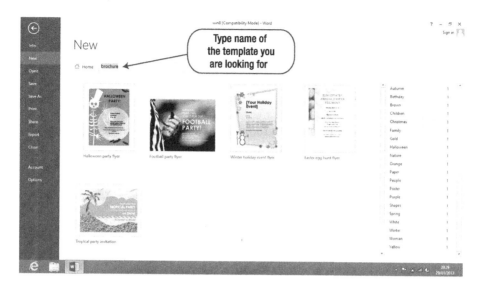

After you select a template, you will see your main work screen.

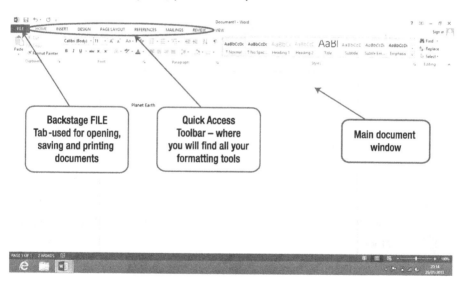

The Ribbon

All the tools used in Microsoft Word are organized on the Ribbon into tabs, loosely based on their function.

The most used tabs are, HOME, INSERT, and PAGE LAYOUT. For normal use of Word, these are the ones you will be using the most.

The HOME Tab

You will find your text-formatting tools here for making text bold, changing the style, font, paragraph alignment, and more.

The INSERT Tab

This is where you will find your clipart, tables, pictures, page breaks, and pretty much anything you would want to insert into a document.

The DESIGN Tab

Here is where you will find anything to do with preset themes and formatting, such as headings, colors, and fonts that you can apply to your document. Word can also automatically format your document according to the themes available.

The PAGE LAYOUT Tab

On this tab, you will find your page sizes, margins, page orientation (landscape or portrait), and anything to do with how your page is layed out.

Basic Text Formatting

When you first open a new document, it looks very plain. We need to format it.

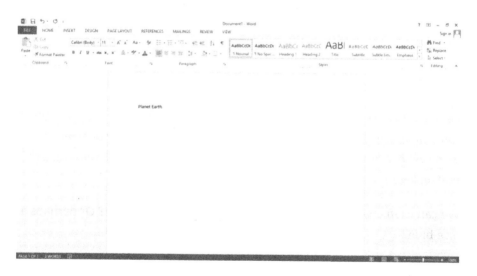

Formatting is done primarily from the HOME tab.

Formatting Tools

Formatting tools are on the HOME tab, shown next.

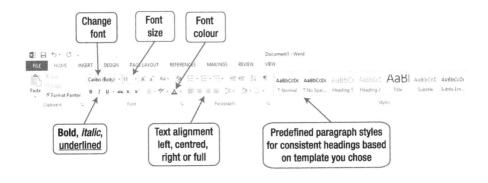

We can change the **font**, the size of the text, whether it is **bold**, *italic*, or underlined.

We can also change the alignment of the text to left aligned, centered, right aligned, or fully justified. Following is an example of fully justified text

Fully justified means it's aligned with both the left and right margins at the same time, which can make paragraphs of text look neater. It only really works on paragraphs like this, so you can see the left and right margins are both in line.

We can even change the color of the text. Maybe a bright red? Or perhaps a nice blue?

Predefined Styles

To format our document, we are going to use the predefined styles.

These are styles that have been already created to allow you to keep consistent-looking headings and text effects in your documents. They also make it easier to apply different font styles and sizes without having to set each individually every time.

So to change the text "Planet Earth" to Title style, highlight the title in your document as shown here.

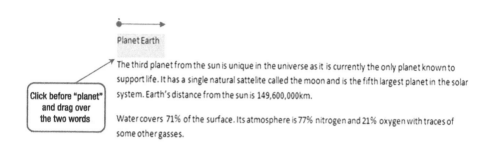

Planet Earth

The third planet from the sun is unique in the universe as it is currently the only planet known to support life. It has a single natural sattelite called the moon and is the fifth largest planet in the solar system. Earth's distance from the sun is 149,600,000km.

Water covers 71% of the surface. Its atmosphere is 77% nitrogen and 21% oxygen with traces of some other gasses.

Click before "planet" and drag over the two words

Next, go to the Styles group in your HOME tab, and click the Title style choice, as shown below.

Planet earth

If I wanted to change the last paragraph to **bold**, I can select the whole paragraph and click the bold button in the Font group of the HOME tab.

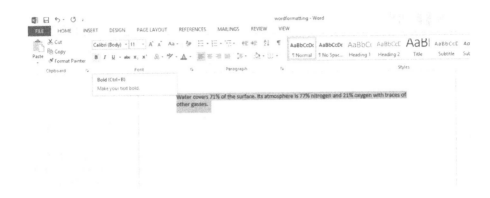

Copy, Cut, and Paste

To ease editing documents, you can use copy, cut, and paste to move paragraphs or pictures around in different parts of your document. For example, in the document shown in the following screen I want to move the second paragraph after the image instead of before it. Simply cut and paste to do this.

First, select the paragraph, with your mouse by clicking before the word "water" and dragging your mouse across the paragraph toward the word "surface" in the same paragraph.

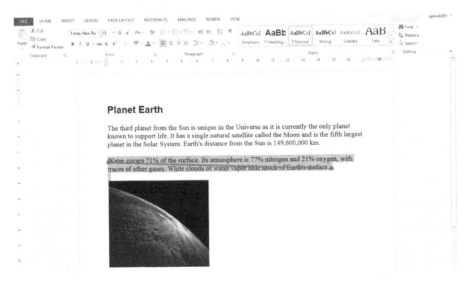

Then click the "Cut" icon in the Clipboard group of the HOME tab.

Enter a space after the image.

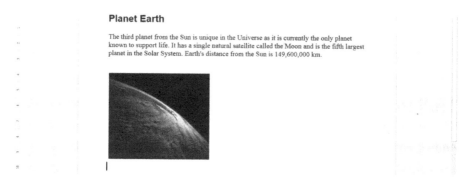

Then click the "Paste" icon in the Clipboard group of the HOME tab.

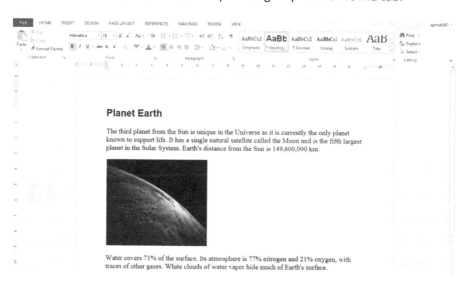

Follow the same method for copy. Remember, though, the copy command makes a copy of the original paragraph, rather than removing it.

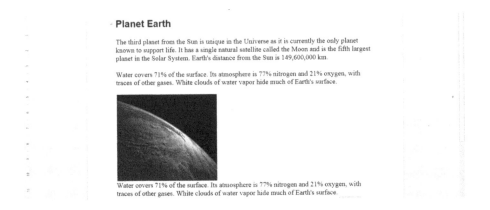

Planet Earth

The third planet from the Sun is unique in the Universe as it is currently the only planet known to support life. It has a single natural satellite called the Moon and is the fifth largest planet in the Solar System. Earth's distance from the Sun is 149,600,000 km.

Water covers 71% of the surface. Its atmosphere is 77% nitrogen and 21% oxygen, with traces of other gases. White clouds of water vapor hide much of Earth's surface.

Water covers 71% of the surface. Its atmosphere is 77% nitrogen and 21% oxygen, with traces of other gases. White clouds of water vapor hide much of Earth's surface.

Adding Images

Adding images to your document is easy. There are two types.

- Your own photos and pictures.

- Clipart. This is a large library of images that can be used in your documents.

The easiest way to add your own photographs or pictures is to find them in your File Explorer window and drag them on top of your document.

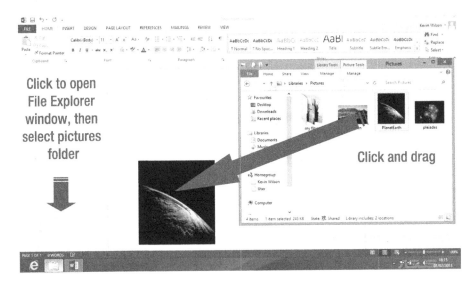

Click to open File Explorer window, then select pictures folder

Click and drag

It helps to position your windows as shown above.

You might need to resize the image. To do this, click on the image, and you'll see small handles appear on each corner of the image. These are called resize handles and you can use them by clicking and dragging a corner toward the center of the image to make it smaller, as shown below.

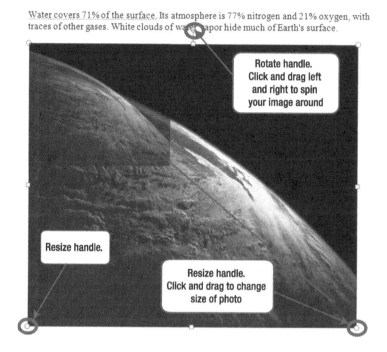

Cropping Images

To crop an image, first drag and drop an image from your "Pictures" library into your document, as shown in the following screen.

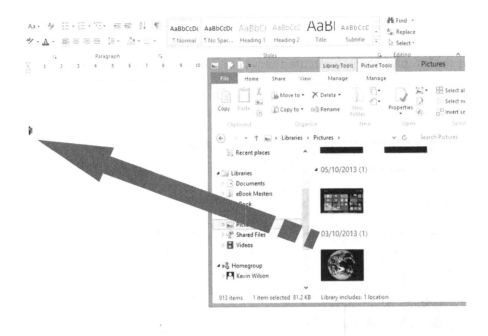

Click on the image and click the FORMAT tab. From the FORMAT tab, click the "Crop" icon in the Size group.

If you look closely at your image, you will see crop handles around the edges of the image.

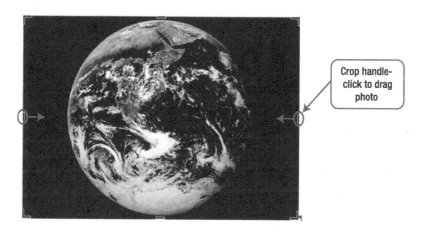

Crop handle- click to drag photo

Click and drag these around the part of the image you want.

The dark grey portions will be removed to leave only the image inside the crop square.

Adding Clipart

To insert clipart, go to your INSERT tab, and click the "Online Pictures" icon in the Illustrations group.

Then type in what you are looking for in the dialog box.

Double-click the picture you want to insert.

World Population

The human population of the world is estimated by the United States Census Bureau to be 6,821,600,000. The world population has been growing continuously since the end of the Black Death around 1400.

Formatting Images

When you click on your image, another tab called PICTURE TOOLS FORMAT appears.

This allows you to add effects and lay out your pictures on your page.

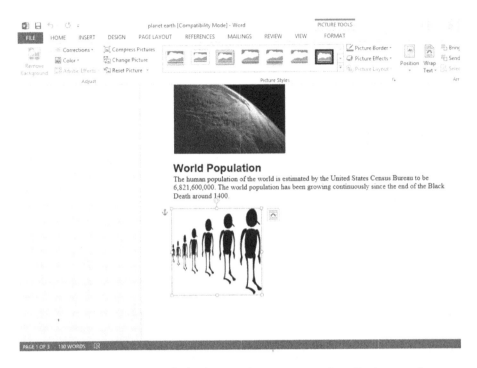

The first thing we want to do is change the text wrapping. Text wrapping enables you to surround a picture or diagram with text.

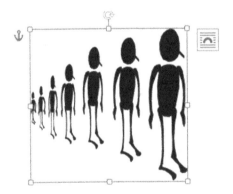

Click on your image, and go to the PICTURE TOOLS FORMAT tab.

Go the Arrange group, and click the "Wrap Text" icon. Then select "Square" from the drop-down menu. This wraps the text squarely around the image. Do this with the photograph as well.

Now you should be able to drag and position your images into the document and have the text wrap itself neatly around the images, as shown below.

Planet Earth

The third planet from the Sun is unique in the Universe as it is currently the only planet known to support life. It has a single natural satellite called the Moon and is the fifth largest planet in the Solar System. Earth's distance from the Sun is 149,600,000 km.

Water covers 71% of the surface. Its atmosphere is 77% nitrogen and 21% oxygen, with traces of other gases. White clouds of water vapor hide much of Earth's surface.

World Population

The human population of the world is estimated by the United States Census Bureau to be 6,821,600,000. The world population has been growing continuously since the end of the Black Death around 1400.

Adding Effects to Images

To add effects to your images, such as shadows and borders, click on your image, and then select the PICTURE TOOLS FORMAT tab.

In this example, click on the planet earth photo. Next, click the "Picture Effects" icon in the Picture Styles group. Select "Shadow" from the drop-down list. Then select an "Outer" shadow, as shown below.

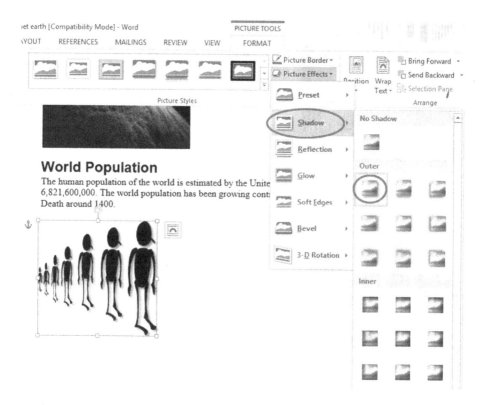

Do this with both images; try a different picture effect on the second image. Perhaps a nice reflection effect.

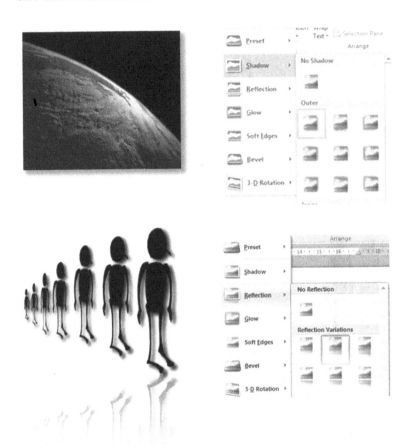

Adding Tables

To insert a table, make sure you click in your document where you want the table to appear. In this example, I want it to appear just below the world population paragraph.

World Population

The human population of the world is estimated by the United States Census Bureau to be 6,821,600,000. The world population has been growing continuously since the end of the Black Death around 1400.

Go to your INSERT tab and select the "Table" icon from the Tables group. In the grid that appears, highlight the number of rows and columns you want. For this table, I chose one row and two columns.

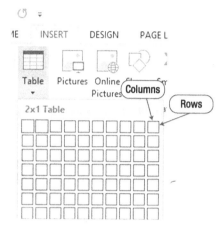

This will add a table with one row and two columns to your document.

World Population

The human population of the world is estimated by the United States Census Bureau to be 6,821,600,000. The world population has been growing continuously since the end of the Black Death around 1400.

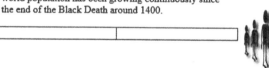

When working with tables, two new tabs appear, TABLE TOOLS DESIGN and TABLE TOOLS LAYOUT.

The TABLE TOOLS DESIGN tab allows you to select preset designs for your table, such as column and row shading, borders, and more.

For this table, I am going to choose one with black headings and gray shaded rows.

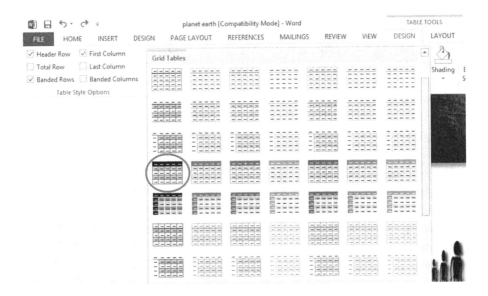

You can now enter the data into your table and Word will shade and format the table for you.

World Population

The human population of the world is estimated by the United States Census Bureau to be 6,821,600,000. The world population has been growing continuously since the end of the Black Death around 1400.

Year	Population (millions)
1960	3
1980	4
1990	5
2000	6
2030	9
2050	12

Saving Your Work

To save your work, click the small disk icon in the top left-hand corner of the screen.

In the Save As screen, you need to tell Word where you want to save the document.

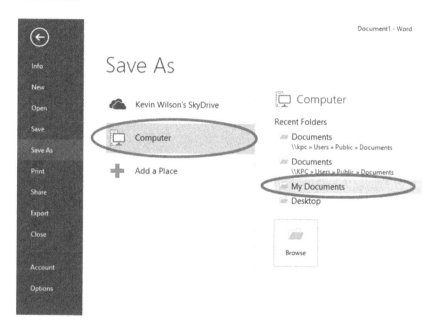

Save it into your Computer > My Documents folder, as shown above. This saves the file to your local computer.

Next, Word will ask you what you want to call the file. Think of a meaningful name describing the work. In this case, "planet earth."

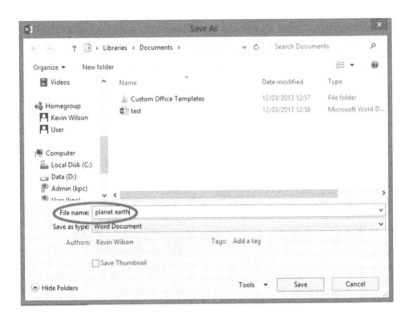

Click the "Save" button.

Printing Your Work

To print your document, click the FILE tab on the top left-hand corner of the screen.

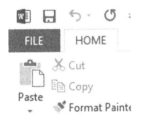

In the following screen, select the correct printer and number of copies you want.

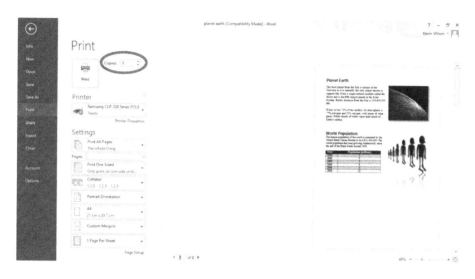

Finally, click the big "Print" icon.

CHAPTER 3

■ ■ ■

Microsoft PowerPoint 2013

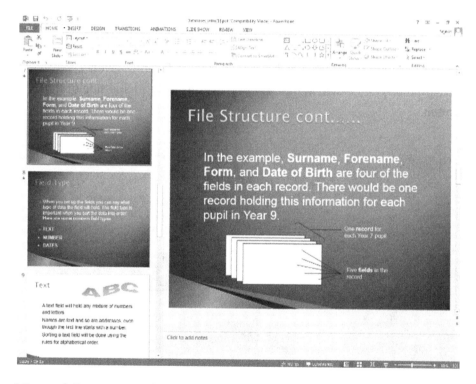

Microsoft PowerPoint allows you to create multimedia presentations.

Starting PowerPoint

To launch PowerPoint, go to the Start screen and select "PowerPoint 2013."

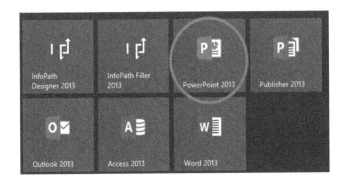

After PowerPoint has loaded, select one of the following templates to start a new presentation or select "Blank Presentation" to start your own. I'm going to go with the "Mesh" template. Your most recently saved presentations are shown in the orange pane on the left-hand side of the screen.

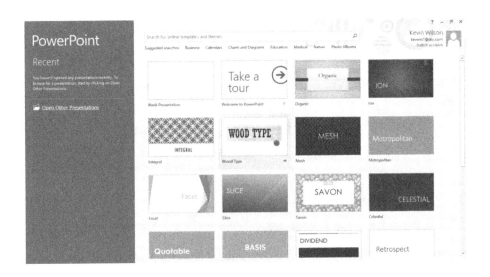

Following is PowerPoint's main screen. The tools are grouped into tabs, according to their function.

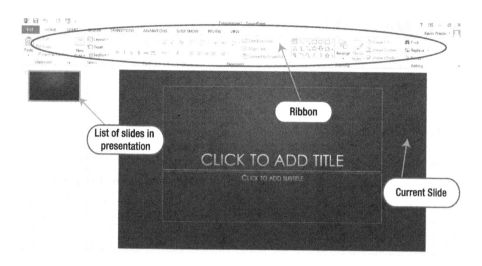

The Ribbon

In PowerPoint, the tools on the Ribbon are arranged in tabs according to their use.

The HOME Tab

The HOME tab is where you will find all the tools to do with text formatting, such as making text bold, changing fonts, or changing the color of the text. These are your most commonly used tools.

The INSERT Tab

This is where you will find all the tools to do with inserting photos, graphics, tables, charts, sounds, movies, and more.

The DESIGN Tab

This is where you will find all the tools to do with the look of your slide, such as the slide background and various themes that are available for quick formatting.

The TRANSITIONS Tab

This is where you will find all the tools that add effects as slides transition from one to the next.

The ANIMATIONS Tab

This is where you will find all the tools to add various animations to slides.

The SLIDESHOW Tab

This is where you will find all the tools to do with setting up your slideshow and running your presentation.

Designing a Slide

In PowerPoint, you can add photos, clipart, charts, diagrams, text, video, sound, and animations to a slide. To better understand the process, let's walk through a quick project.

Adding a Photo to a Slide

Start by changing the arrangement of the objects on the following slide. You might notice that the image is on top of the text box.

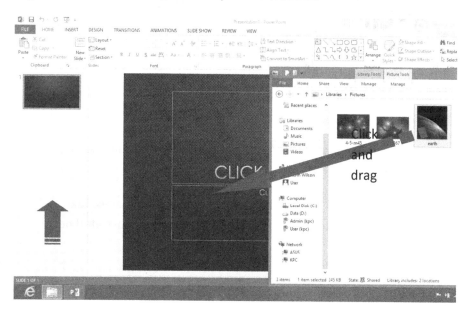

We need to bring the text box to the front, so click the title text box and on your HOME tab, in the Drawing group, click the "Arrange" icon. Then choose "Bring to Front," as shown in the following screen.

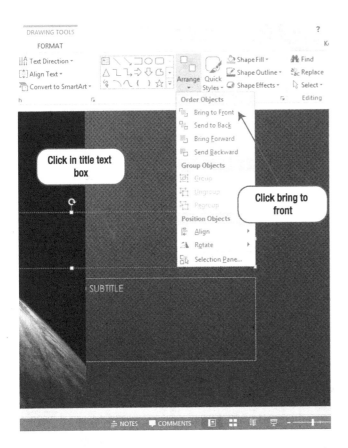

You can now add an appropriate title in the title text box; in this case, "PLANET EARTH."

PowerPoint constructs slides in layers. This means that images, text, and other elements are placed one on top of each other, as illustrated here.

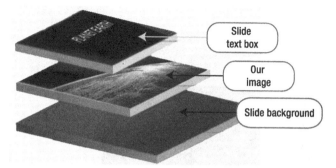

These items, all arranged in layers, create the slide. Here you see the completed slide.

Resizing Images

You can resize an image to fill the whole slide by clicking on the image and dragging the resize handles to the edge of the slide.

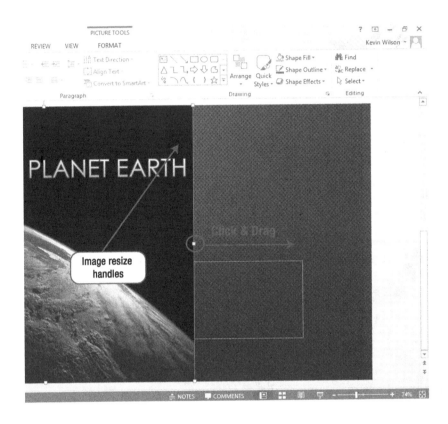

Adding a New Slide

On the HOME tab, in the Slides group, click the "New Slide" icon. Choose "Title and Content" from the resulting options.

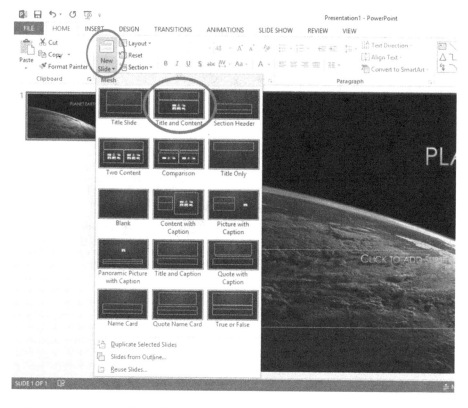

In the next screen, click "CLICK TO ADD TITLE."

Then type the title "COMMON FACTS."

Next, click "Click to add text."

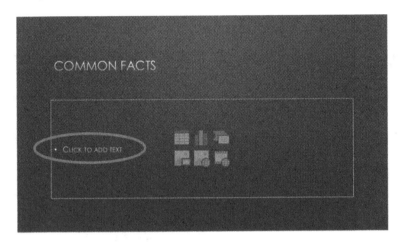

Add the text in the following slide.

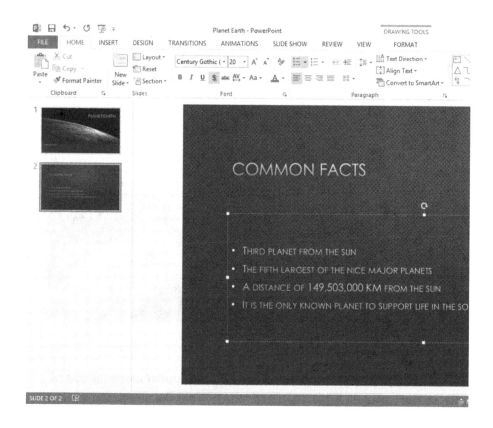

Cropping Images

Add the planet earth image again to the slide by dragging and dropping it from your "Pictures" library to your slide, as shown in the next screen.

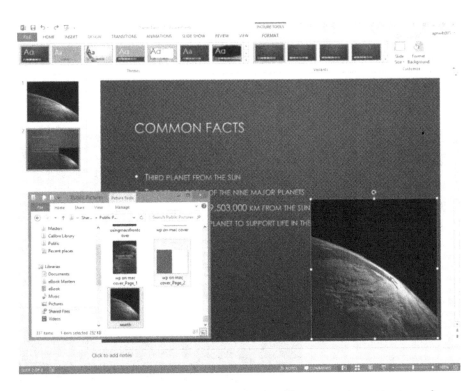

Click the image you want to crop. A new tab will appear along the top of your screen called PICTURE TOOLS FORMAT. From the Size group, click the "Crop" icon.

Click and drag the crop handles so the crop border is around the part of the image you want to keep.

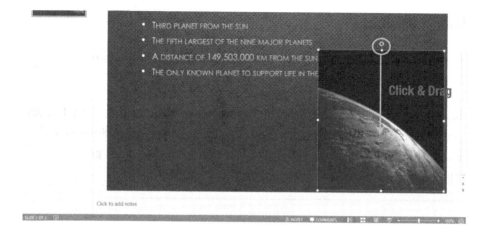

You can then position your image where you want it in your slide. In this example, I have moved it to the bottom.

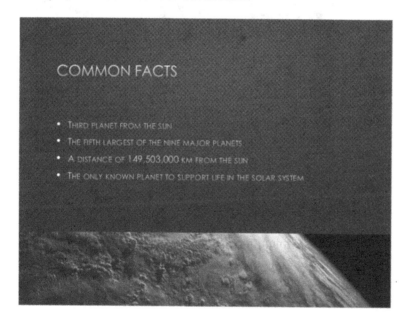

Adding Special Effects

Slide transitions and slide animations are two special effects that will enhance your presentation.

45

Slide Transitions

A slide transition is an animation or effect that is displayed when you move from one slide to the next.

To add transitions to PowerPoint slides, you need to go to the TRANSITIONS tab. On the left-hand pane, click the slide you want to add, and then click one of the transition effects from the "Transition to This Slide" group. In the following scree, "None" is selected.

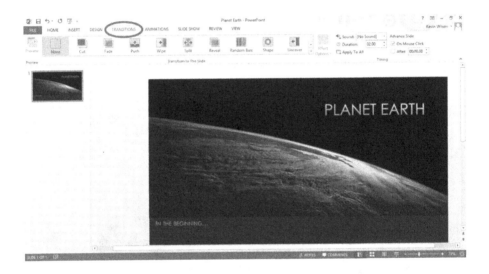

Slide Animations

To demonstrate simple slide animations, we will create a slide in which bullet points appear one at a time instead of all at once. First, select the ANIMATIONS tab from the Quick Access Toolbar. Next, click on the text box containing the bullet points.

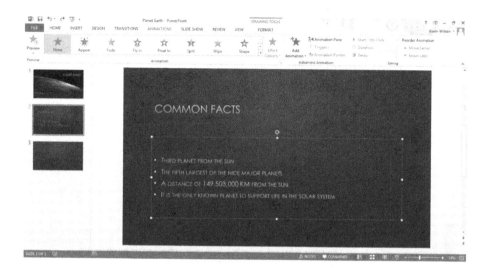

From the Animation group, click the "Appear" icon. This tells PowerPoint you want the points to appear one at a time. You can change how you want them to appear by clicking the "Effect Options" icon.

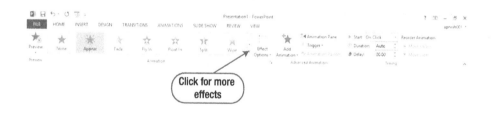

Click for more effects

To view your presentation, press the F5 key on the keyboard.

Press Enter or click your mouse to advance a slide.

Inserting a Table

From the INSERT tab, click the "Table" icon. A drop-down menu containing a grid of squares will appear. Hover the mouse over the grid to select the number of columns and rows you want in your table.

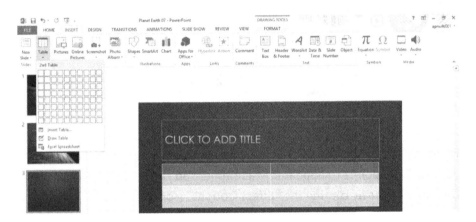

Click a cell in the table to insert the table, and then add your text to the cells.

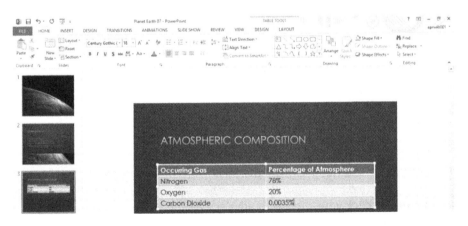

You can also format your table using PowerPoint's predesigned templates. Make sure your table is selected and click the DESIGN tab at the top of your screen. This will open a special TABLE TOOLS DESIGN tab. From here, select one of the templates.

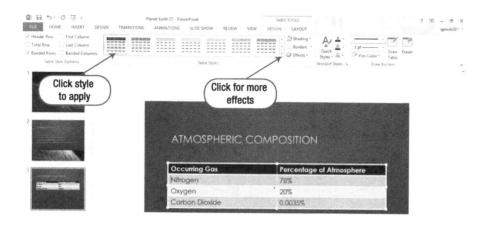

Adding a Chart

From the INSERT tab, in the Illustrations group, click the "Chart" icon. Select a category from the left pane and review the charts that appear in the right pane. Select "Pie" for this example, and click the "OK" button.

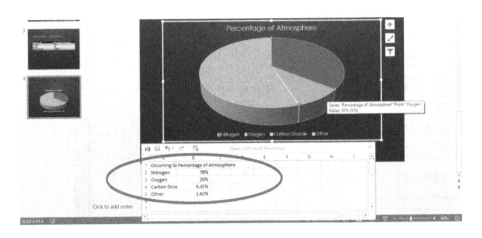

Saving Your Work

To save your work, click the small disk icon in the top left-hand corner of the screen.

In the Save As screen, choose where you want to save the document. In this case, I have chosen the Computer > My Documents folder, as shown in the following screen.

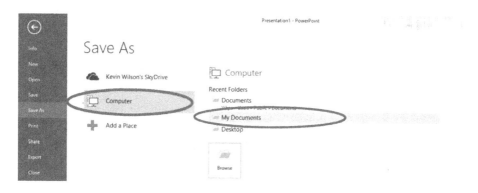

PowerPoint will ask you what you want to call the file. Think of a meaningful name describing the work. In this case, "planet earth."

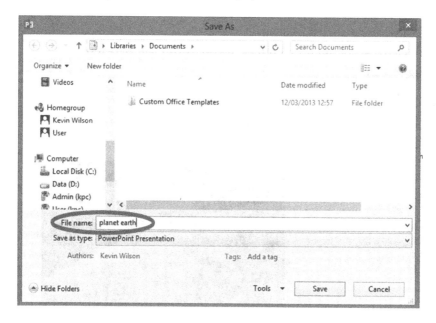

Finally, click the "Save" button.

Printing Your Work

To print your document, go to the FILE tab on the top left-hand corner of the screen.

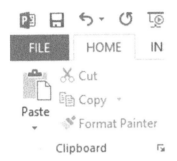

Select the correct printer and number of copies you want, as shown in the following screen.

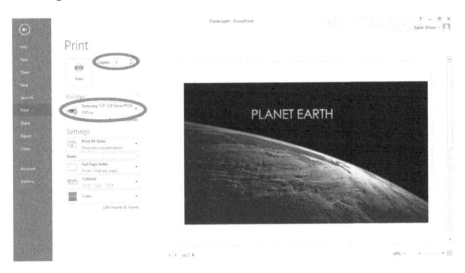

Then select how you want the presentation to print out. Click where it says "Full Page Slides."

This allows you to arrange more than one slide per page, and includes space to write notes. This is useful if you are giving a copy of your slides to your audience, so they can follow your presentation as you speak and take notes.

A good rule of thumb is to print three slides per page, with writing space next to each, as shown here.

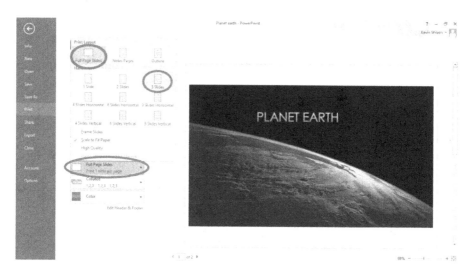

Following is a print preview of what it looks like. Click the "Print" icon to print your presentation.

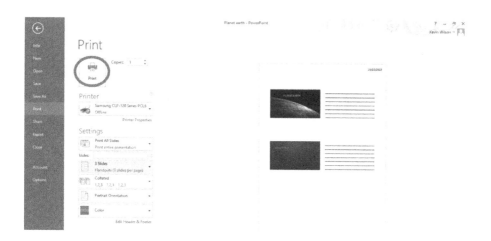

Giving Presentations

When giving your presentations, you will likely use a projector and a laptop.

Setting Up

It's best to make sure both your laptop and projector are turned off before you start.

If the projector cable has a VGA connector, then you will need the adapter.

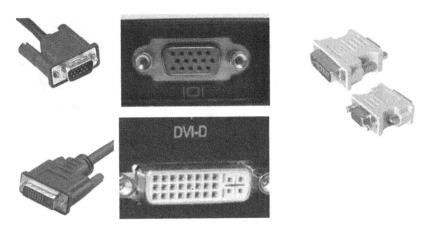

Plug one end of the adapter into the laptop as shown in the next image. It can be inserted only one way.

Plug the other end of the adapter into the projector.

If you are using our projector, plug the other end of the projector cable into the "VGA in" port on the back of the projector.

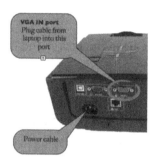

The "VGA in" port is where the cable from the laptop plugs into; it is usually color-coded dark blue. On some projectors it's called "Computer in."

If you are using a ceiling-mounted projector in a classroom or boardroom, you don't usually have to worry about plugging in the cable on the projector.

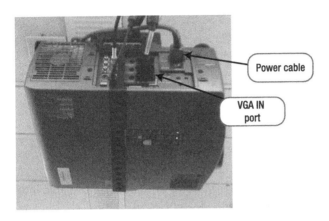

Plug in the power and press ON/STANDBY on the projector.

Make sure the correct input is selected; on most modern projectors, this is automatic. If not, there is usually a button on the projector labeled "Input" or "Source," as shown in the following image. Press repeatedly until the computer is displayed on the projector screen.

Tip   Switch on the projector first, and then turn on the laptop. This allows the laptop to automatically detect the projector.

On most laptops, there is a function key to press if you are not getting any signal. Press and hold FN while pressing F8 (sometimes F5, depending on the model of laptop). The key will have CRT/LCD or a picture of a screen.

And that's all there is to it. You are now ready to give your presentation.

CHAPTER 4

■ ■ ■

Microsoft Excel 2013

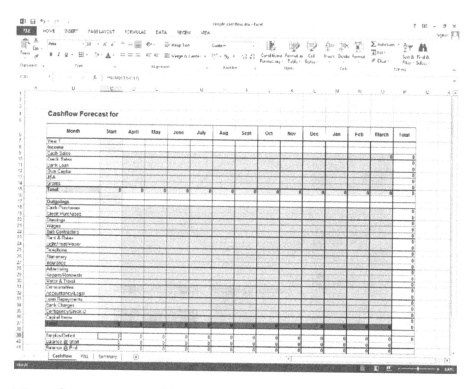

Microsoft Excel is a spreadsheet program that allows you to store, organize, and analyze information.

Starting Excel

To launch Excel, go to the Start screen and select "Excel 2013."

After Excel has loaded, click the File tab and select "New."

Select "Blank workbook" under the available templates. It will be highlighted by default.

A new, blank workbook appears in the Excel window.

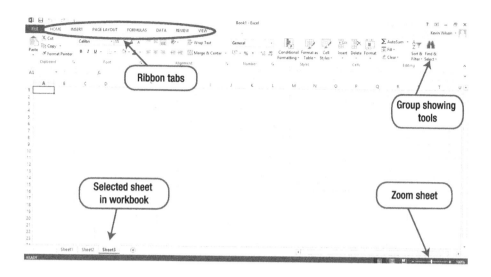

What Is a Spreadsheet?

A spreadsheet is made up of cells, each identified by a reference.

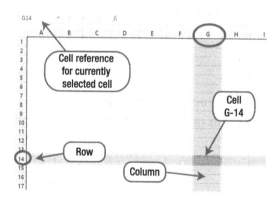

You can also select multiple cells at the same time. A group of cells is called a cell range.

You can refer to a cell range using the cell reference of the first cell and the last cell in the range, separated by a colon. For example, in the following screen, the cell range would be A1:D12.

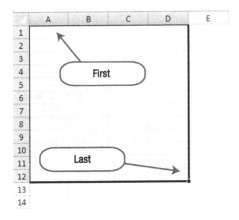

The Ribbon

All the tools used in Microsoft Excel are organized on the Ribbon into various tabs, loosely based on their function.

The most used tabs are, HOME, INSERT, PAGE LAYOUT, FORMULAS, and VIEW. For normal use of Excel, these are the ones you will be using the most.

The HOME Tab

This is where you will find your most used tools, such as basic text formatting, cell borders, cell formatting for text or numbers or currency, and much more.

The INSERT Tab

This is where you will find all your objects you can insert into your spreadsheet, such as shapes, tables, and charts.

The PAGE LAYOUT Tab

This is where you will find your page-formatting functions, such as size of paper, paper orientation when printed, page margins, and more.

The FORMULAS Tab

This is where you will find your formulas, functions, and your data-manipulation tools, such as sum functions, average, counting tools, and more.

The VIEW Tab

This is where you will find your view layouts, where you can zoom into your spreadsheet, among other functions.

Entering Data

In this example, we are creating a basic scoring sheet.

First, we type our data into the appropriate cells on the spreadsheet.

	22-Apr	29-Apr	06-May	13-May	20-May	27-May	03-Jun	10-Jun	17-Jun	24-Jun	01-Jul	08-Jul
Barbara	21	19	21	21	12	21	13	21	9	11	21	18
Ann	10	21	8	21	5	21	10	21	18	21	6	19
Flo	7	7		8		18	6	4		17	12	12
Emily		0	1		21	21	20	9	11			
Josie	21	21	6		7	12	4		3		12	7
Lin									4		9	4
Joan	19			16	12	0			15	14	15	15
Eva	21	14	21	18	21			5		10		21

Inserting Rows and Columns

To insert a new row between the "Flo" and "Emily" rows, right-click with your mouse on the "Emily" row; in this case, row 5.

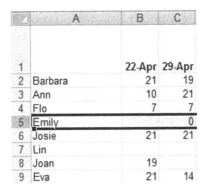

From the menu, click "Insert."

This inserts a blank row as the new row 5.

		22-Apr	29-Apr
1		22-Apr	29-Apr
2	Barbara	21	19
3	Ann	10	21
4	Flo	7	7
5			
6	Emily		0
7	Josie	21	21
8	Lin		
9	Joan	19	
10	Eva	21	14

Resizing Rows and Columns

Resize a column or row by clicking and dragging the column or row divider lines.

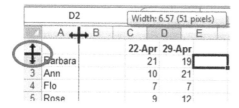

Double-click on these lines to automatically size the row or column to the data that is in the cell.

Using Formulas

Using formulas allows you to perform some calculations on the data you have entered. You can add (total), multiply, subtract, find averages, or plot charts of lists of data, all depending on what your spreadsheet is analyzing.

Adding a Formula to One Row

For example, to add all the scores in my score sheet, I could add another column called "Total" and include a formula to add up the scores for the two weeks the players played.

To do this, I need to find the cell references for Barbara's scores. Her scores are in row 2 and columns B and C.

So the cell references are B2 for her score of 21, and C2 for her score of 19. All formulas begin with an equal sign (=), so in this case the formula is =B2+C2.

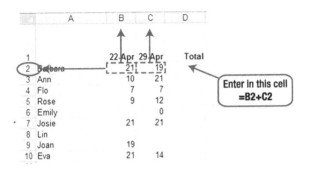

The result is shown in the next figure.

		22-Apr	29-Apr	Total
1				
2	Barbara	21	19	40
3	Ann	10	21	
4	Flo	7	7	
5	Rose	9	12	
6	Emily		0	
7	Josie	21	21	
8	Lin			
9	Joan	19		
10	Eva	21	14	

Adding a Formula to Muliple Rows

You can replicate this formula for the rest of the players without having to type it in multiple times.

On the selected cell, there is a small square on the bottom right-hand side, as shown here.

Click on this and drag it with your mouse down the rest of the column.

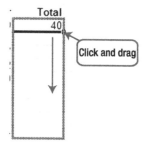

Excel will automatically copy the formula and calculate the rest of the totals for you.

		22-Apr	29-Apr	Total
1				
2	Barbara	21	19	40
3	Ann	10	21	31
4	Flo	7	7	14
5	Rose	9	12	21
6	Emily		0	0
7	Josie	21	21	42
8	Lin			0
9	Joan	19		19
10	Eva	21	14	35

Using Functions

A function is a predefined formula. Excel provides over 300 different functions, all designed to make analyzing your data easier. We will start with some basic, everyday functions.

Let's say we wanted to add up the number of games played automatically. We could do this with a function.

First, we need to insert a new column after the "29-Apr" column. Right-click on the column, and from the menu, click "Insert."

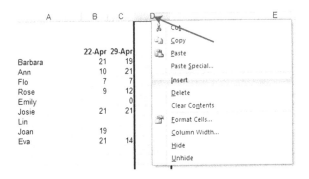

Call the column "Played," as shown in the following image.

	22-Apr	29-Apr	Played	Total
Barbara	21	19		40
Ann	10	21		31
Flo	7	7		14
Rose	9	12		21
Emily		0		0
Josie	21	21		42
Lin				0
Joan	19			19
Eva	21	14		35

From the FILE tab, click "Insert Function."

In the Insert Function dialog box, select the "COUNT" function from the list, and then click the "OK" button.

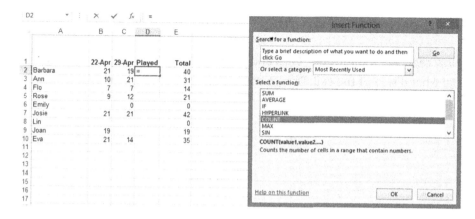

Now we need to tell the COUNT function what we want it to count. We want to count the number of games played. Barbara's scores are in cells B1 and C1, so highlight these two by dragging your mouse over, as circled in the following image.

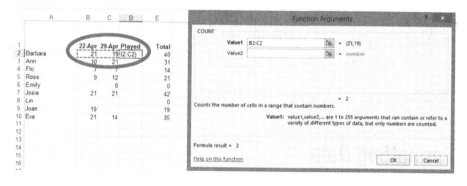

Click the "OK" button. You can see she has played two games.

	A	B	C	D	E
1		22-Apr	29-Apr	Played	Total
2	Barbara	21	19	2	40
3	Ann	10	21		31
4	Flo	7	7		14
5	Rose	9	12		21
6	Emily		0		0
7	Josie	21	21		42
8	Lin				0
9	Joan	19			19
10	Eva	21	14		35

Replicating the Formula

Now replicate the formula. Click and drag the small square on the bottom right-hand side of the cell. Drag it down over the rest of the columns.

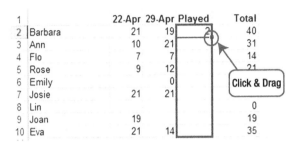

As shown here, Excel has automatically calculated the totals.

	22-Apr	29-Apr	Played	Total
2 Barbara	21	19	2	40
3 Ann	10	21	2	31
4 Flo	7	7	2	14
5 Rose	9	12	2	21
6 Emily		0	1	0
7 Josie	21	21	2	42
8 Lin			0	0
9 Joan	19		1	19
10 Eva	21	14	2	35

Formatting Data

In Excel, there are different types of data to consider, such as numbers, currencies, and text.

In the next two sections, we'll format data according to numbers and currencies.

Averaging Numbers

In this example, we are going to work out the average scores over the number of games the players have played. Let's review how now.

First, insert another column and call it "Average," as shown here.

	22-Apr	29-Apr	Played	Total	Average
Barbara	21	19	2	40	
Ann	10	21	2	31	
Flo	7	7	2	14	
Rose	9	12	2	21	
Emily		0	1	0	
Josie	21	21	2	42	
Lin			0	0	
Joan	19		1	19	
Eva	21	14	2	35	

In this case, the formula would be total number of games played divided by total score. To create this formula, we will use the following symbols:

Multiply	*
Divide	/
Add	+
Subtract	-

Use the forward slash for divide (/), as shown in the next image.

	A	B	C	D	E	F
1		22-Apr	29-Apr	Played	Total	Average
2	Barbara	21	19	2	40	=E2/D2
3	Ann	10	21	2	31	
4	Flo	7	7	2	14	
5	Rose	9	12	2	21	
6	Emily		0	1	0	
7	Josie	21	21	2	42	
8	Lin			0	0	
9	Joan	19		1	19	
10	Eva	21	14	2	35	

Unfortunately, the number format isn't as accurate as we want it. We need to tell Excel that the data in this column is a number accurate to two decimal places.

First, click and drag over the column of numbers to highlight it.

71

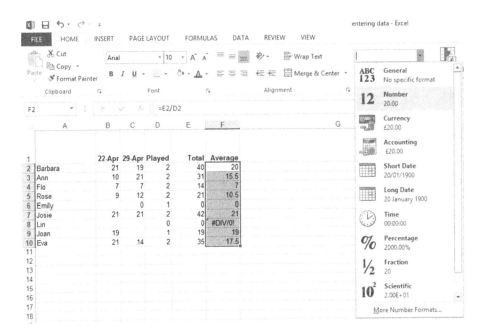

On the HOME tab, go to the Number format group, and click the drop-down menu to show your formatting choices.

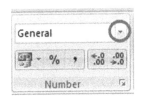

From the drop-down menu, click "Number," as shown here.

Recording Fees

It would be the same procedure if we were, for example, recording the fees paid by the players.

Insert another column and call it "Fee." Say the fees are 9 British pounds. When we enter 9 into the column, Excel thinks it's just a number, so we need to tell Excel that it is currency.

	22-Apr	29-Apr	Played	Total	Average	Fee
Barbara	21	19	2	40	20.00	9
Ann	10	21	2	31	15.50	9
Flo	7	7	2	14	7.00	9
Rose	9	12	2	21	10.50	9
Emily		0	1	0	0.00	9
Josie	21	21	2	42	21.00	9
Lin			0	0	#DIV/0!	9
Joan	19		1	19	19.00	9
Eva	21	14	2	35	17.50	9

Select all the data in the "Fee" cell. Go back to the HOME tab, and click the drop-down arrow in the Number group to select the Number format.

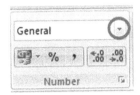

This time, select "Currency" from the drop-down menu.

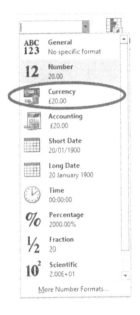

This will format all the numbers as a currency.

	22-Apr	29-Apr	Played	Total	Average	Fee
Barbara	21	19	2	40	20.00	£9.00
Ann	10	21	2	31	15.50	£9.00
Flo	7	7	2	14	7.00	£9.00
Rose	9	12	2	21	10.50	£9.00
Emily		0	1	0	0.00	£9.00
Josie	21	21	2	42	21.00	£9.00
Lin			0	0	#DIV/0!	£9.00
Joan	19		1	19	19.00	£9.00
Eva	21	14	2	35	17.50	£9.00

Adding a Chart

The easiest way to add a chart is to select from your spreadsheet a column you want for the x axis and a column you want for the y axis.

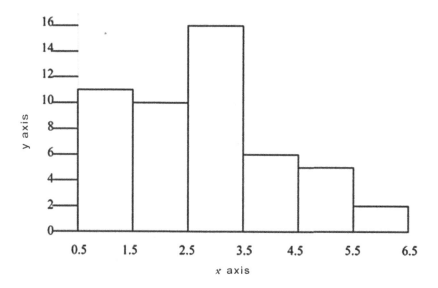

Let's create a chart for the total scores. First, select all the names in the first column. This will be the x axis on the chart.

Now hold down the Ctrl key on your keyboard. This allows you to multi-select. While holding Ctrl, select the data in the "Total" column. This will be the y axis on the chart. Note that the data in the names column is still highlighted.

		A	B	C	D	E		
E1					f_x	Total		

Click & Drag

	A	B	C	D	E		
		22-Apr	29-Apr	Played		Total	Average	Fee
1		22-Apr	29-Apr	Played		Total	Average	Fee
2	Barbara	21	19	2		40	20.00	£9.00
3	Ann	10	21	2		31	15.50	£9.00
4	Flo	7	7	2		14	7.00	£9.00
5	Rose	9	12	2		21	10.50	£9.00
6	Emily		0	1		0	0.00	£9.00
7	Josie	21	21	2		42	21.00	£9.00
8	Lin			0		0	#DIV/0!	£9.00
9	Joan	19		1		19	19.00	£9.00
10	Eva	21	14	2		35	17.50	£9.00
11								

Release the Ctrl key and go to the INSERT tab. In the center of the tab, you will find some different types of charts, including line charts, column charts, and pie charts. Let's choose a 3D column chart, so click on the 3D column icon.

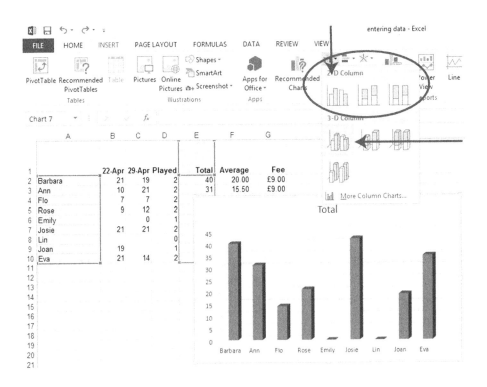

You are automatically taken to the design tab where you can select a style to auto-format the chart for you. Select a style that looks good; for example, a shaded effect.

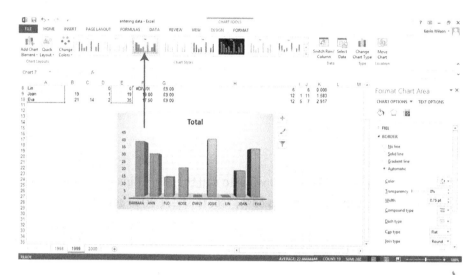

Saving Your Work

To save your work, click the small disk icon in the top left-hand corner of the screen.

In the Save As screen, choose where you want to save the document. Save it to the Computer > My Documents folder, as shown in the following image.

Next, Excel will ask you what you want to call the file. Think of a meaningful name describing the work. In this case, "score sheet 2013 season."

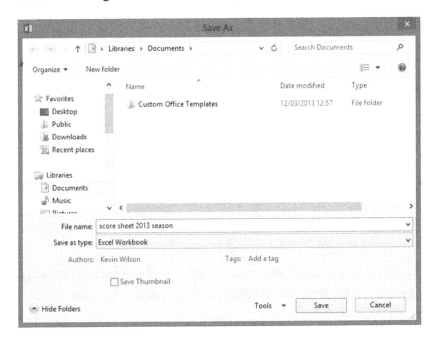

Click the "Save" button.

Printing Your Work

To print your document, click the FILE tab on the top left-hand corner of the screen.

In the following screen, select the correct printer and number of copies you want.

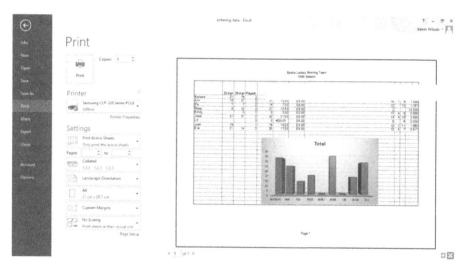

Finally, click the big "Print" icon button.

CHAPTER 5

■ ■ ■

Microsoft Outlook 2013

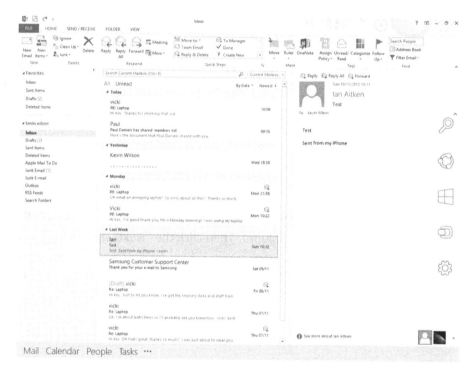

Mail Calendar People Tasks •••

Microsoft Outlook allows you to send and receive e-mail, record appointments using the calendar feature, maintain your contacts in address books, and much more.

Setting Up Outlook

When you first start the Outlook application, you will be asked to enter your e-mail address, password, and possibly your mail settings.

On the Welcome screen, click the "Next" button, then select the "Yes" option to the question "Do you want to set up Outlook to connect to an email account?" Then click the "Next" button to continue.

On the resulting Add Account screen, enter your name, e-mail address, and password for your Office 365 account. Then click the "Next" button to continue.

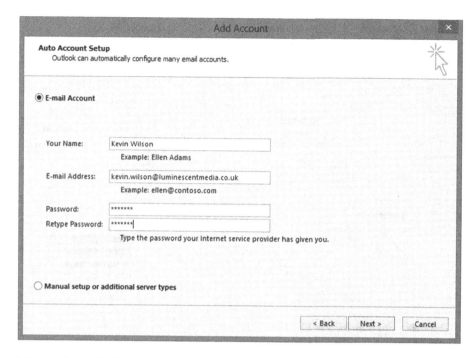

Microsoft Outlook will locate the e-mail address you have supplied and enter all the server and mail settings for you.

Getting Started with Outlook

When you start Outlook, you will see the following main screen. I've highlighted the main features you need to know in order to get started quickly and easily.

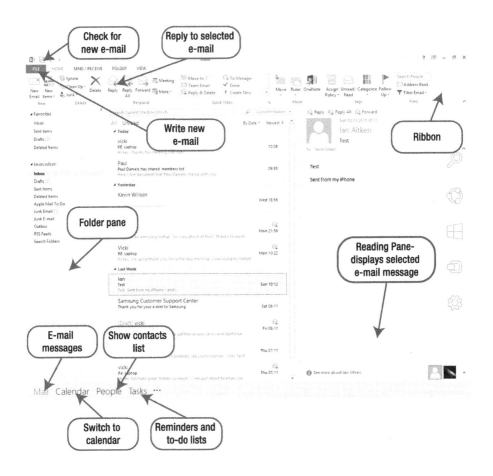

The Ribbon

All the main features and functions of Outlook are organized on the Ribbon into various tabs.

The FILE Tab

This is where you can find all your print, save, export, and account settings.

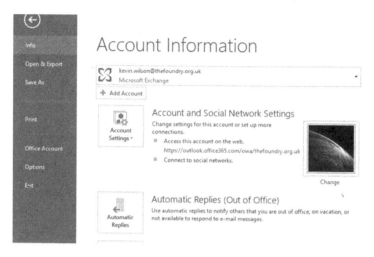

The HOME Tab

This is where you will find all your most used features, such as composing new e-mails, reply, and delete functions.

The SEND/RECEIVE Tab

This is where you will find all your functions for manual sending and receiving of e-mail. Most of the time, you won't need to use these, except when you want to manually send or receive new e-mails.

The FOLDER Tab

The FOLDER tab is where you will find functions to create folders for organizing your e-mails. For example, perhaps you would want a folder for "Vicki" to house all e-mails from Vicki, or a folder for "Accounts" for all e-mails from your accounting or banking services.

The VIEW Tab

The VIEW tab allows you to sort your e-mails by name or date, and allows you to turn on or off different sections, such as the reading pane.

Sending E-mail

From the HOME tab, in the New group, click the "New Email" icon.

In the window that appears, enter the e-mail address of your recipient in the "To" field. When you start typing in the address, Outlook will search your contacts and display suggested addresses.

You can also add e-mail addressed by clicking the "To" field and selecting the recipients from your address book. Note that you may select more than one if you want to send the same message to other people.

The "Cc" field stands for carbon copies and is used to send a copy of the message to other people.

The "Bcc" field stands for blind carbon copies. This works like the Cc field, except the recipient can't see the addresses of the other people the message has been sent to.

After you have filled out the necessary fields, type your message at the bottom.

You can also send attachments, such as photos or documents. To do this, click on the "Attach File" icon that looks like a paper clip. Select your file from the resulting Insert File dialog box, and click the "Insert" button. You can select more than one file by holding down the Ctrl key on your keyboard, as shown in the following screen on the right.

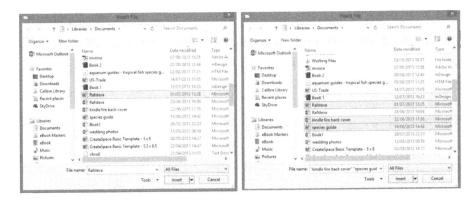

Once you are happy with your message, click the "Send" button.

Organizing Your E-mails with Rules

Rules can save you a lot of time by automatically moving messages as they arrive. For example, if you always move e-mails from a certain person to a certain folder, you could create a rule to do this automatically. You can create rules that look for a specific sender, recipient, subject, or specific words that are contained in the body of the e-mail.

Creating a New Rule

From the HOME tab, in the Move group, select the "Rules" icon.

Select "Manage Rules & Alerts..." from the drop-down menu.

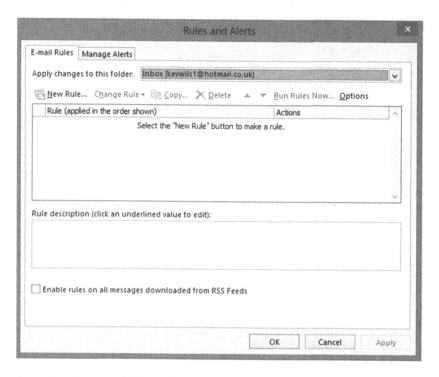

From the Rules and Alerts dialog box, click the "New Rule..." option. This will bring up the Rules Wizard. To automatically move messages that come in from a certain person, click "Move messages from someone to a folder." Then click the "Next" button.

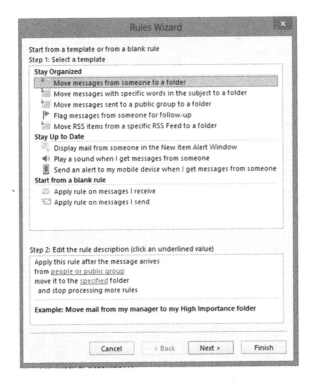

To move messages from someone, select "from people or public group" in Step 1.

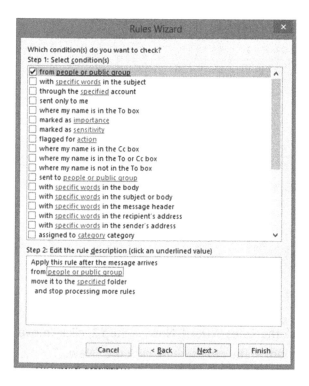

Select the e-mail address and click the "From ->" button. Then click the "OK" button.

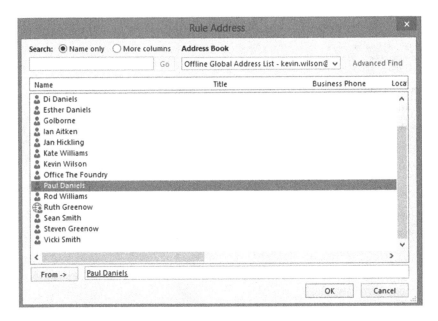

You will then be brought back the Rules Wizard. Now, in Step 2, click "move it to the specified folder" option. In the next screen, click the "New…" button to create a new folder. In the dialog box that appears, type in the name of your folder and select "Inbox" to create the new folder in your inbox.

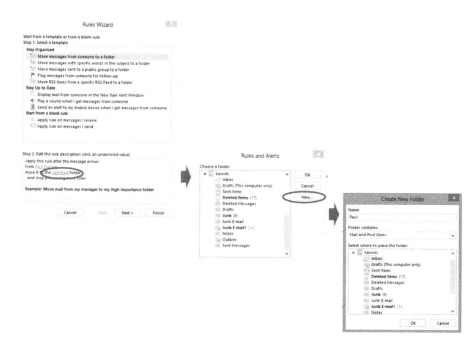

After you are done, click the "OK" button. All e-mails received from that e-mail address will be automatically placed in this folder. This can be very useful if you have e-mail from a lot of people.

Getting Started with the Calendar

To start the Calendar, click the calendar icon located at the bottom left of your main Outlook screen.

Once you are in your calendar, you can see how it is set up with months and dates. It is personal preference, but I find it easier to work within month view. To do this, go to the HOME tab, and within the Arrange group, click on the "Month" icon, as shown in the following screen. The quickest way to add an event or appointment is to double-click the day.

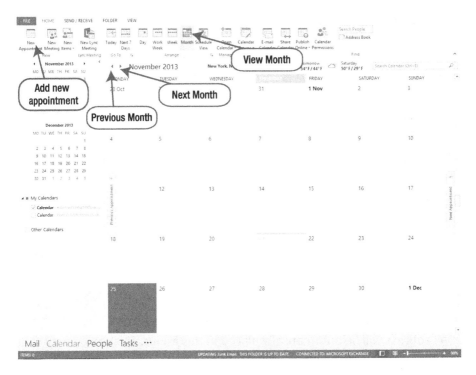

So, for example, if you wanted to add an appointment on the 25th, double-click on the 25 square.

This would bring up the following dialog box. Remove the check mark from "All day event" to allow you to enter a specific start time and end time.

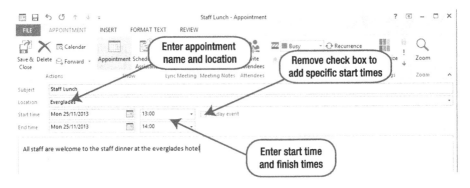

In the following calendar, you can see the appointment has been added.

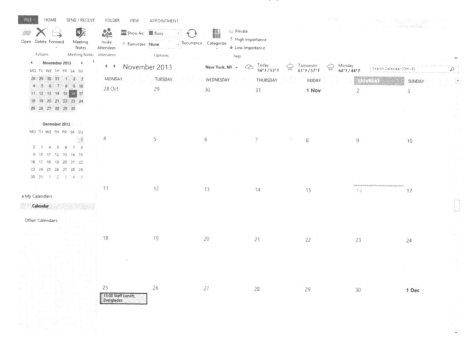

Get the eBook for only $10!

Now you can take the weightless companion with you anywhere, anytime. Your purchase of this book entitles you to 3 electronic versions for only $10.

This Apress title will prove so indispensible that you'll want to carry it with you everywhere, which is why we are offering the eBook in 3 formats for only $10 if you have already purchased the print book.

Convenient and fully searchable, the PDF version enables you to easily find and copy code—or perform examples by quickly toggling between instructions and applications. The MOBI format is ideal for your Kindle, while the ePUB can be utilized on a variety of mobile devices.

Go to www.apress.com/promo/tendollars to purchase your companion eBook.